The Gigantic Turnip

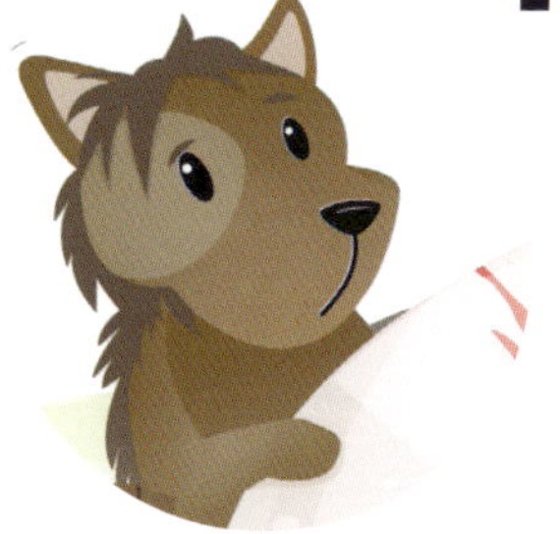

Written by
Stephen Rickard

Illustrated by
Heike Jane Zimmermann

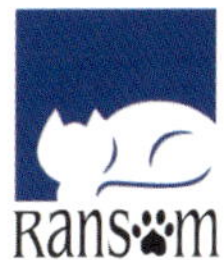

Ransom

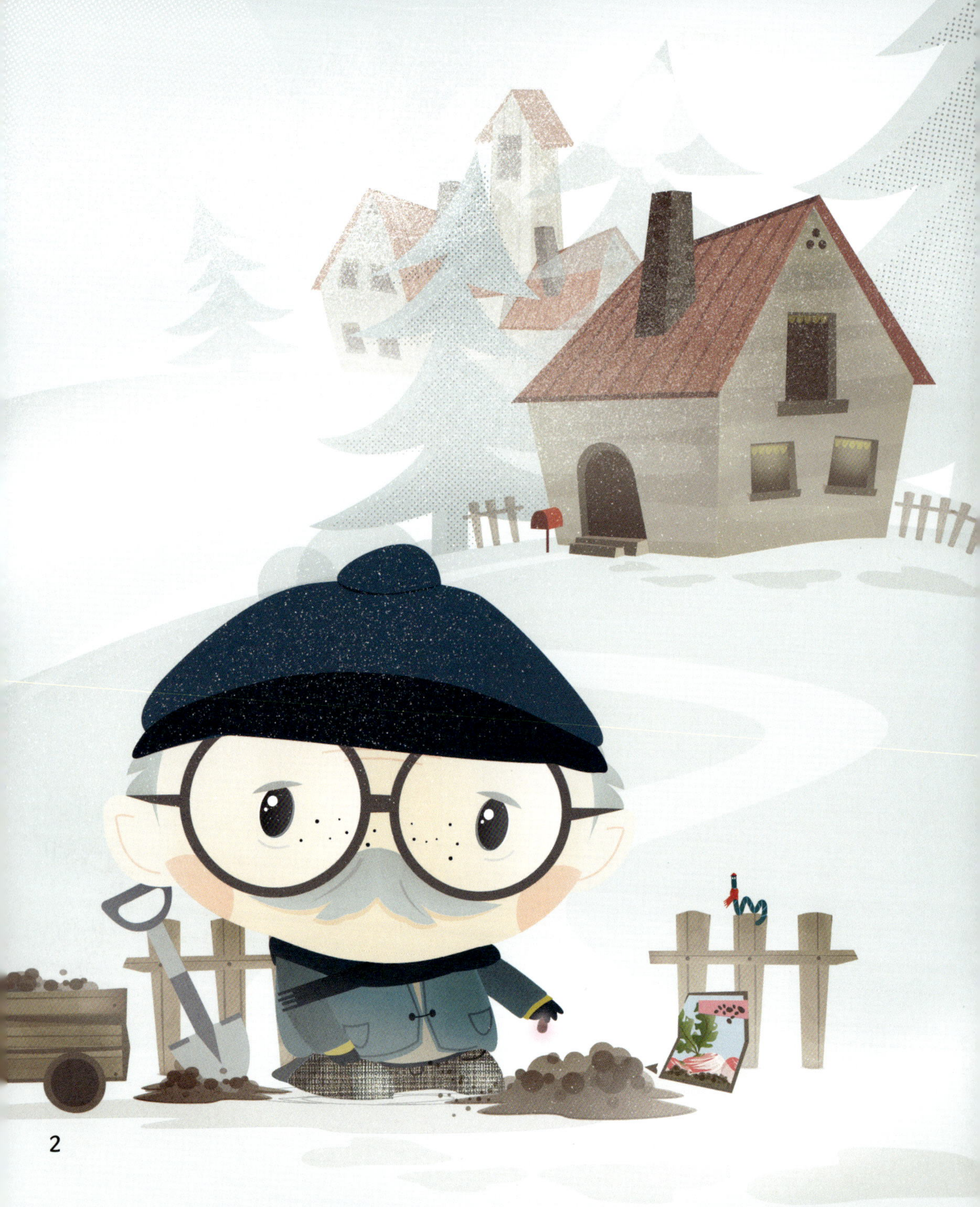

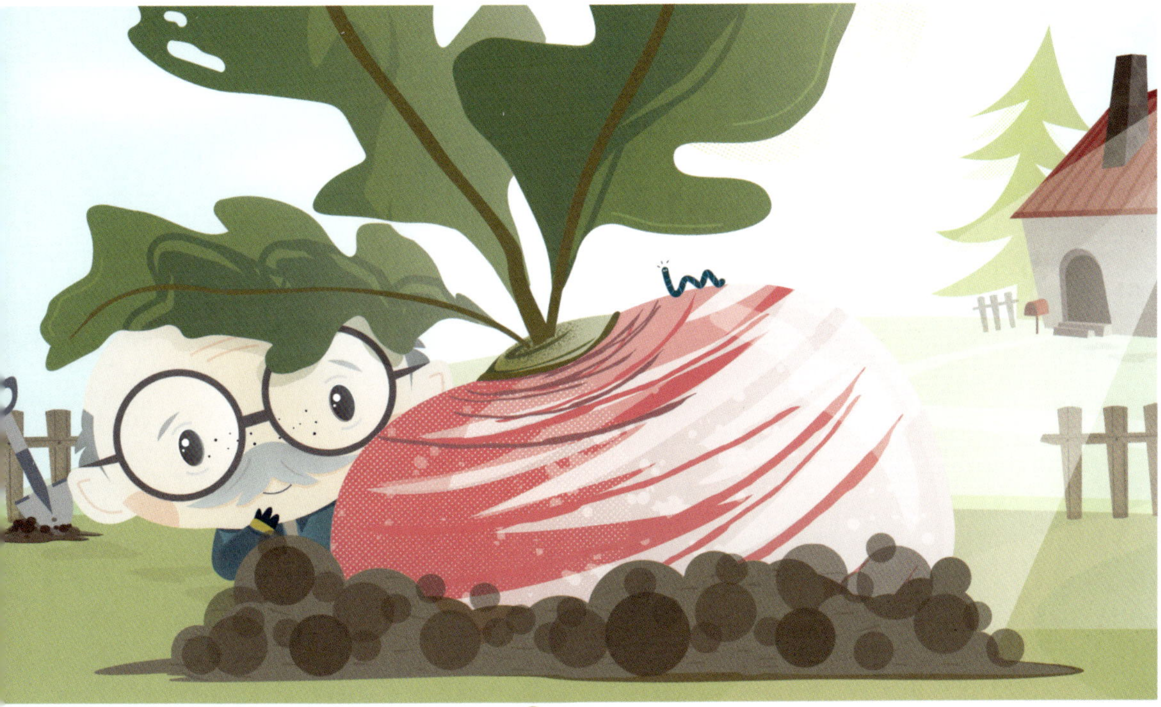

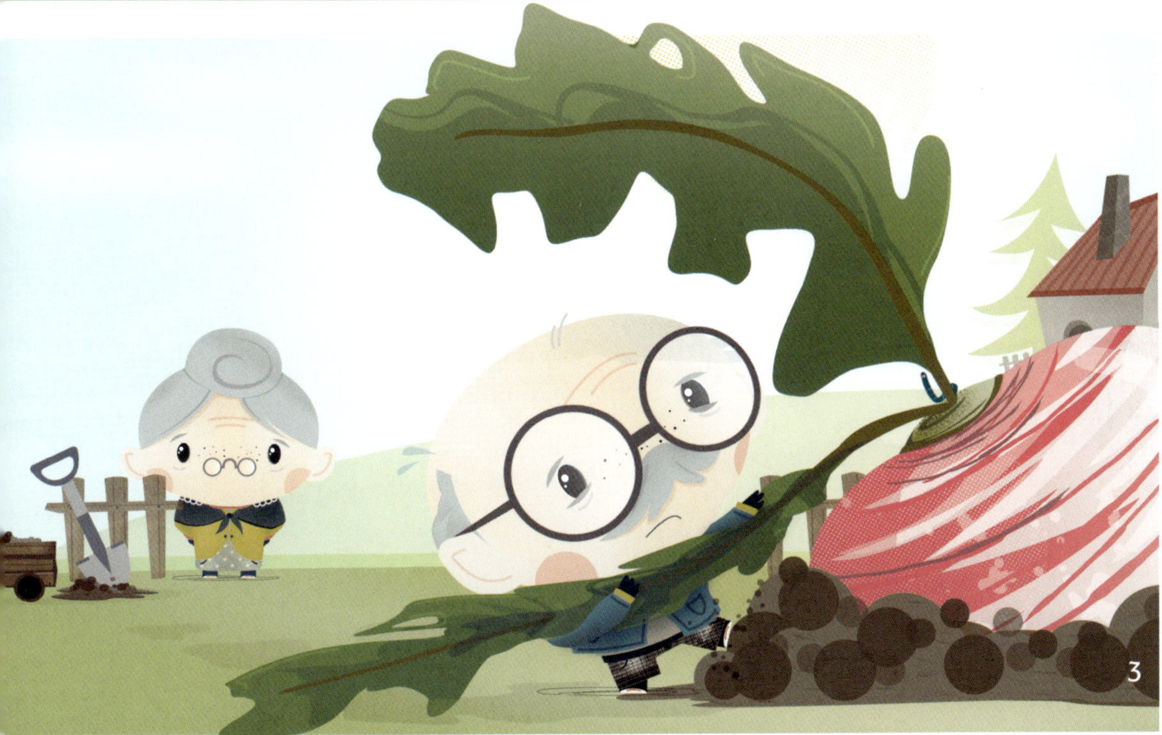

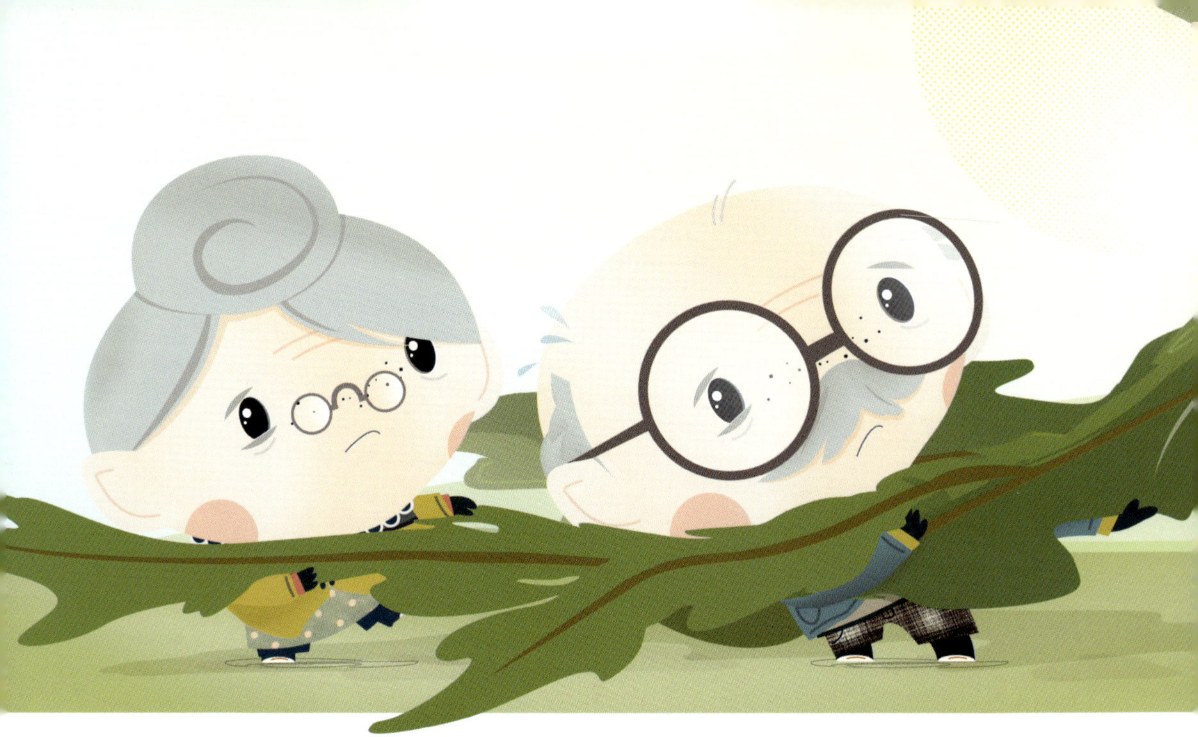

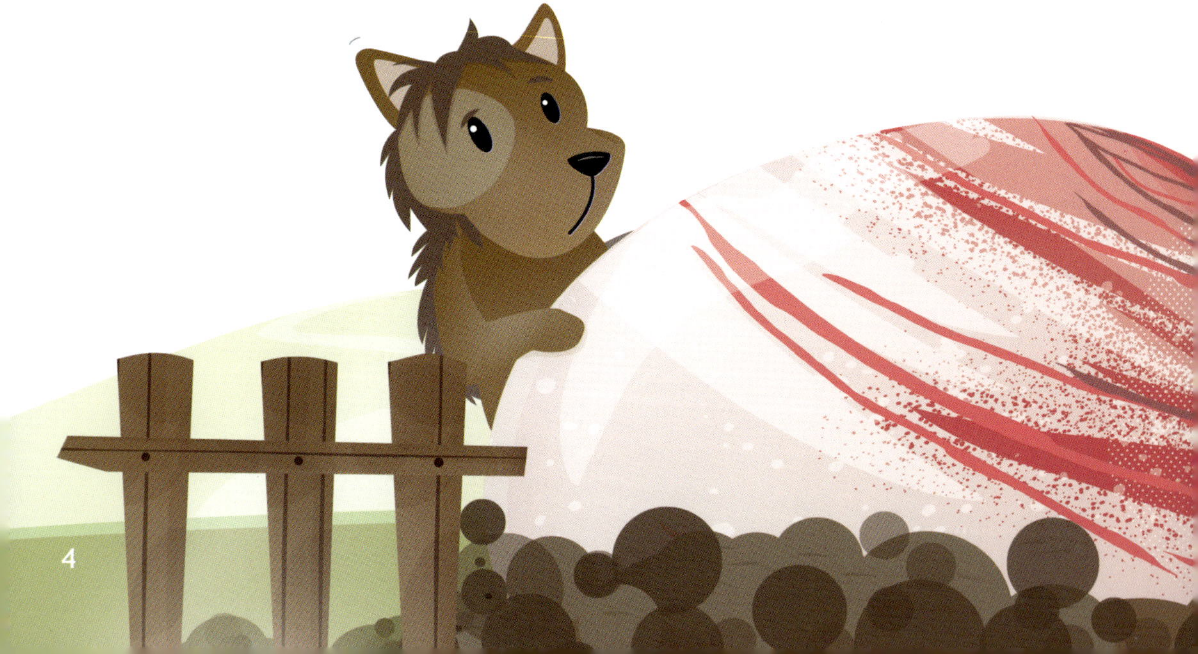

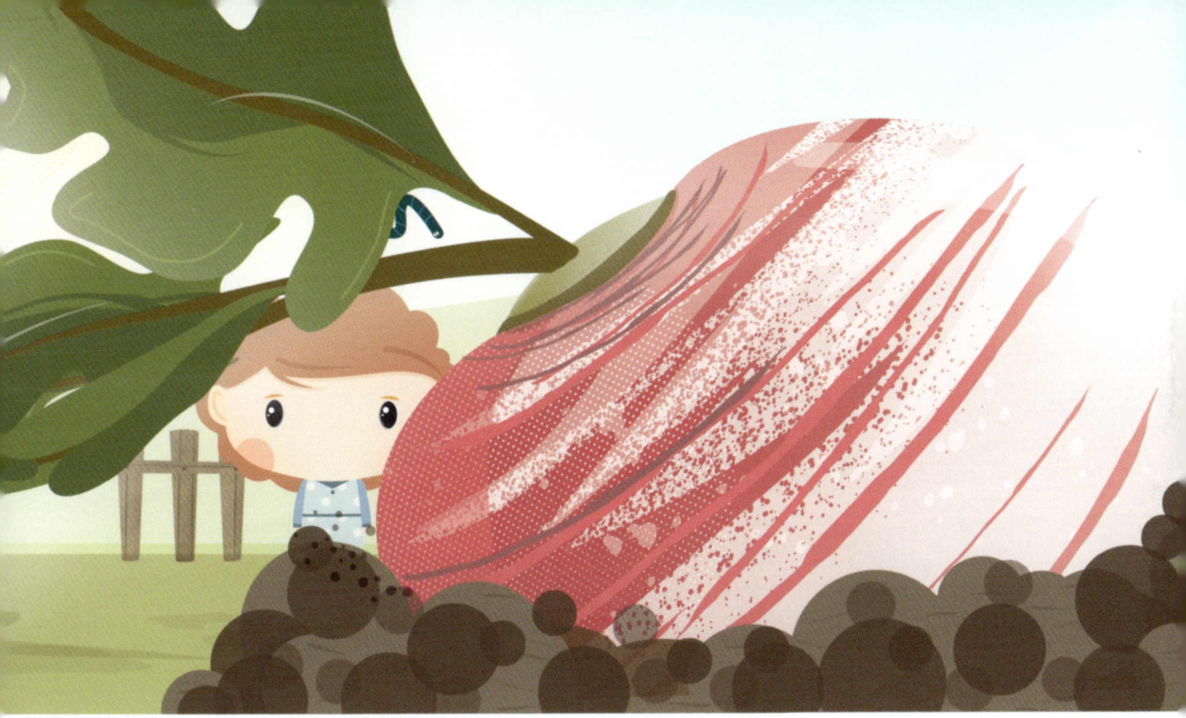

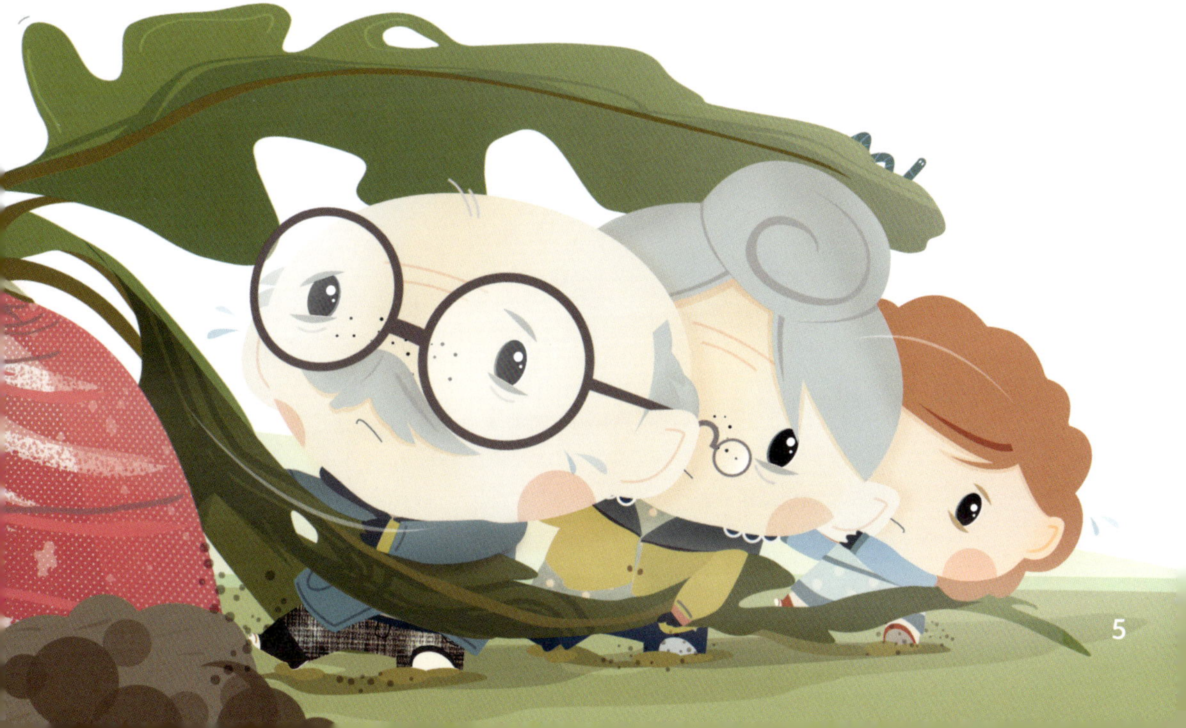

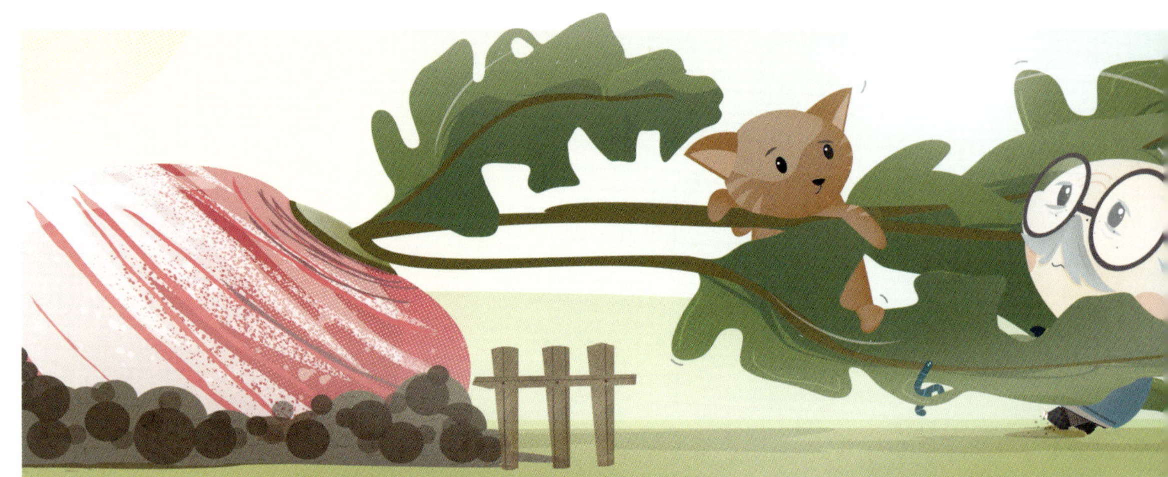

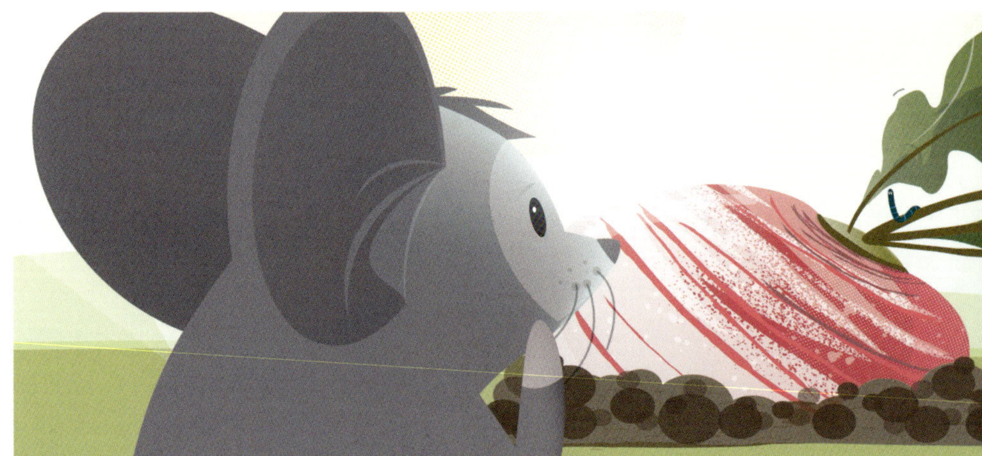

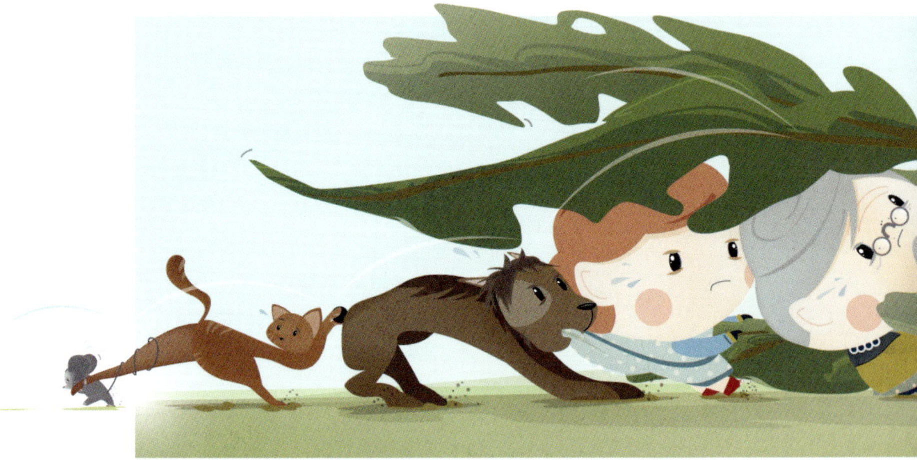

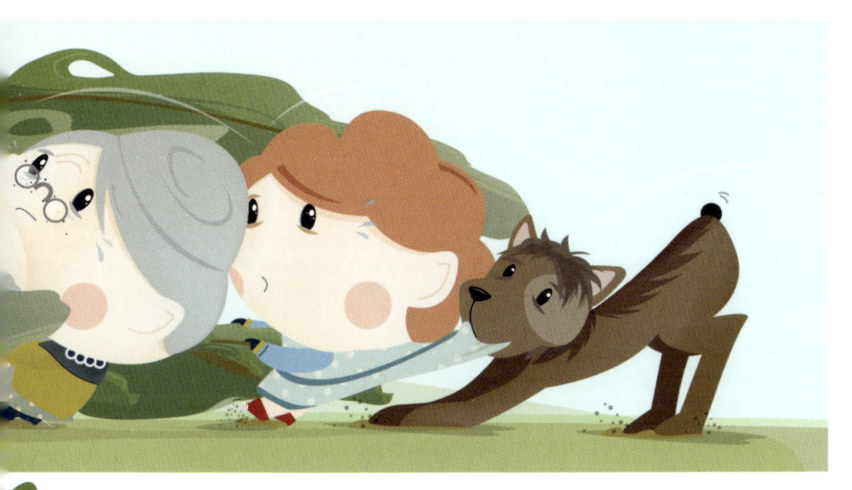

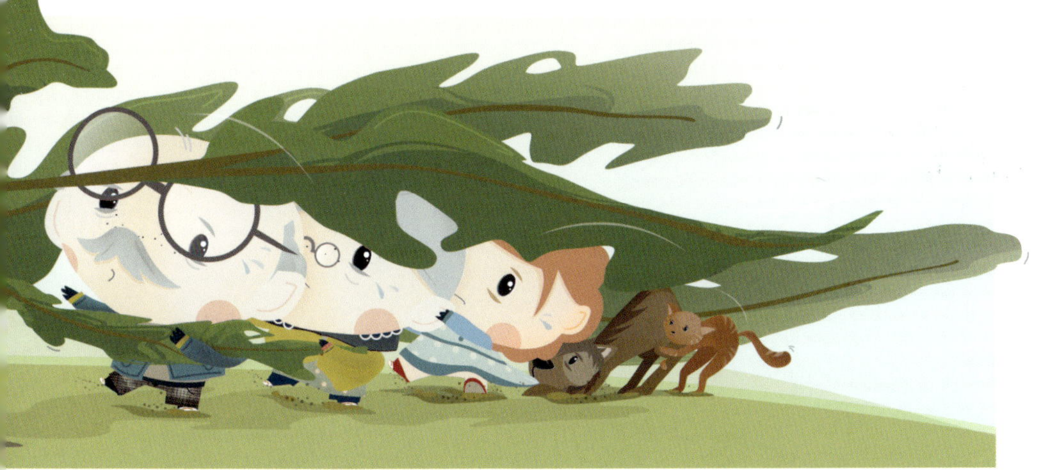

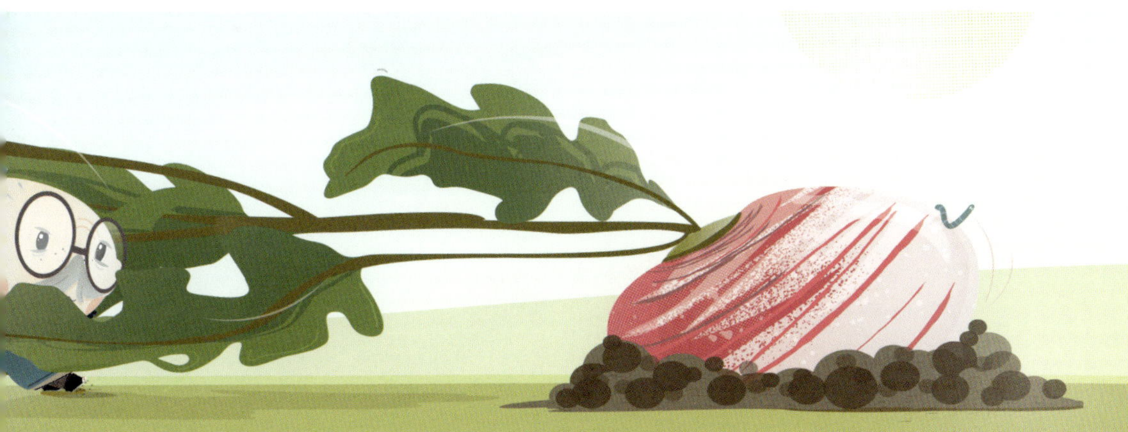

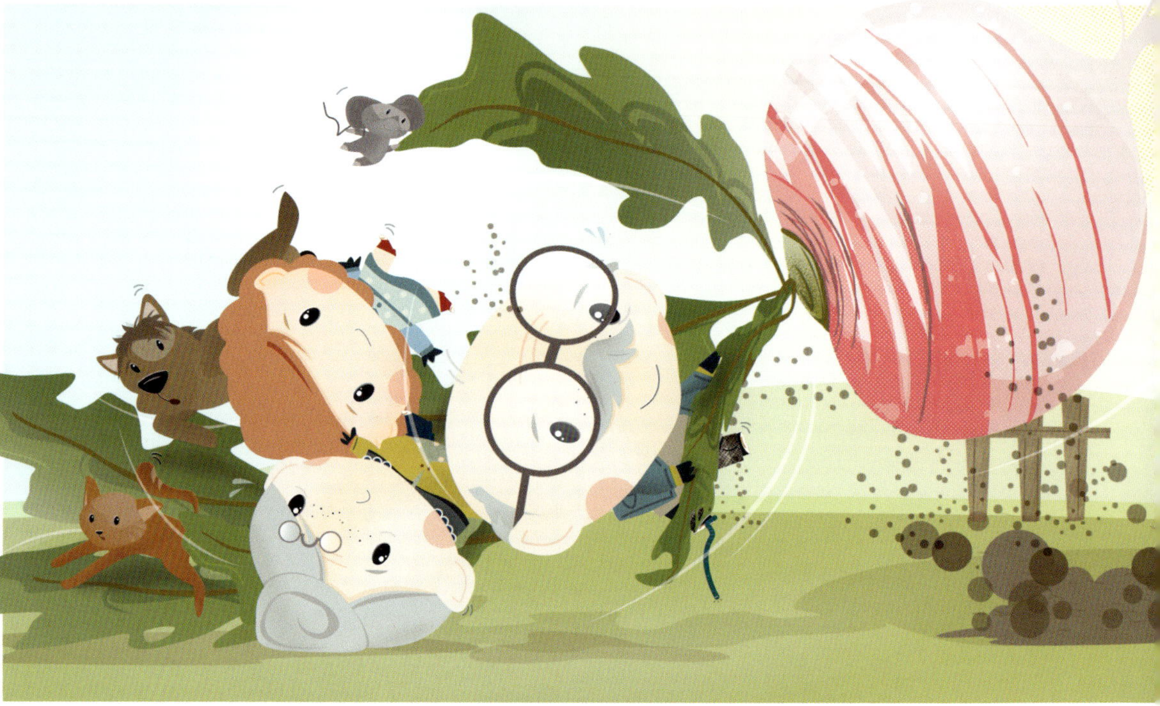

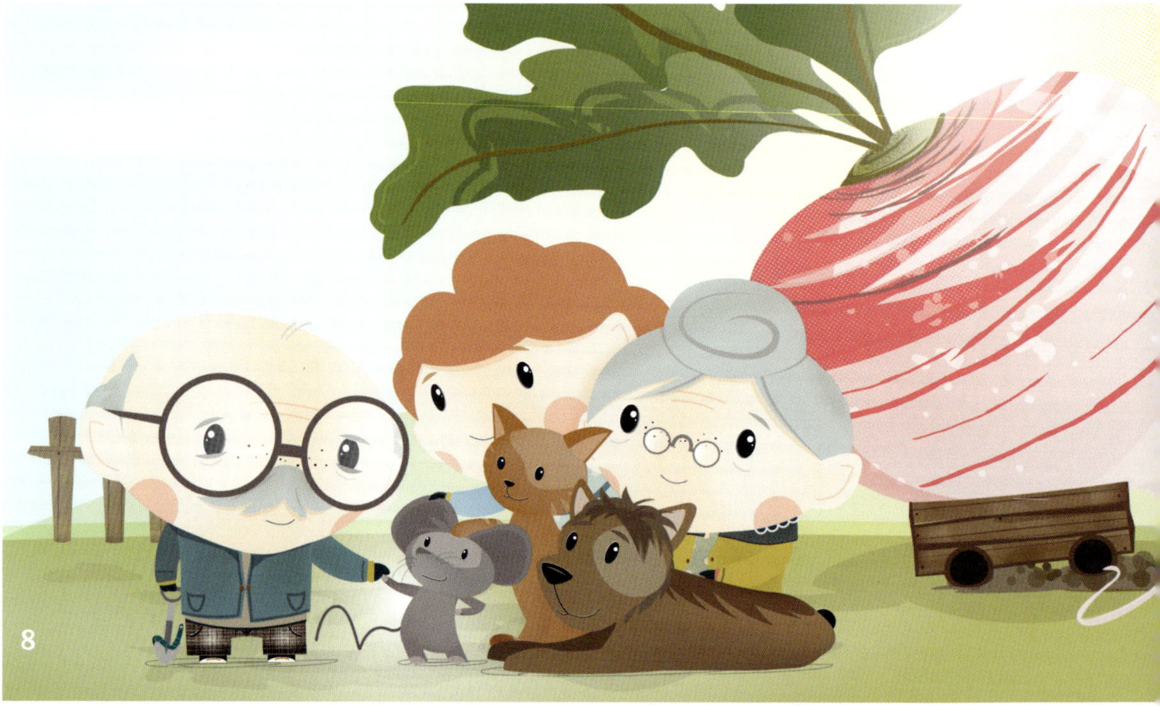